WHY ALLIGATORS
MAKE GOOD GOLFERS

WHY ALLIGATORS MAKE GOOD GOLFERS

A GUIDE TO THICK SKIN AND MENTAL TOUGHNESS

DR. MARK F. FRAZIER, PSY.D.

iUniverse, Inc.
New York Lincoln Shanghai

WHY ALLIGATORS MAKE GOOD GOLFERS
A GUIDE TO THICK SKIN AND MENTAL TOUGHNESS

Copyright © 2006 by Mark F. Frazier

All rights reserved. No part of this book may be used or reproduced by any means, graphic, electronic, or mechanical, including photocopying, recording, taping or by any information storage retrieval system without the written permission of the publisher except in the case of brief quotations embodied in critical articles and reviews.

iUniverse books may be ordered through booksellers or by contacting:

iUniverse
2021 Pine Lake Road, Suite 100
Lincoln, NE 68512
www.iuniverse.com
1-800-Authors (1-800-288-4677)

ISBN-13: 978-0-595-39626-9 (pbk)
ISBN-13: 978-0-595-84029-8 (ebk)
ISBN-10: 0-595-39626-7 (pbk)
ISBN-10: 0-595-84029-9 (ebk)

Printed in the United States of America

To
Brittney and Kevin

Contents

INTRODUCTION ix
PLAYING WITH CONFIDENCE 1
CONCENTRATING COMPLETELY 11
MANAGING NERVOUSNESS 19
OVERCOMING FRUSTRATION 27
THE PRE-SHOT ROUTINE 35
THINKING STRAIGHT 45
CONCLUSION 69
BIBLIOGRAPHY 73

INTRODUCTION

We've arrived at the most important part of the game...how to play golf from the shoulders up.

—Arnold Palmer

It may surprise you, but alligators play golf. That's right. They play golf. In fact, they're quite good. You probably haven't seen them play, but that's because they tee up at night. The darkness doesn't affect their vision, the courses are wide open, and the sprinklers are on, so their skin stays nice and moist. Speaking of skin, that's one reason alligators make good golfers. Their skin is thick. And in this sport, that's a big advantage.

Another reason alligators make good golfers is their mastery of the mental side of the game. Alligators understand that golf is a test of physical and mental skills. Throughout their careers, gators spend about half the time working on the physical side of their game. The other half is dedicated to the mental side. This is not the case with human golfers. Humans spend all of their time working on the physical side of their game, focusing exclusively on grip, stance, takeaway, and downswing. They will tell you that the mental side is important. But if you ask a group of humans to explain how a golfer develops his mental skills, there's usually a long silence before someone confesses, "I don't know."

The mental side of golf is as important as the physical side. Just ask Bobby Jones and Jack Nicklaus.

Bobby Jones practiced very little. Months would go by, and he wouldn't even touch his clubs. Other players would sharpen their games before the season started, but Jones preferred to wait until the first tournament and then play his way into shape. Before a round, he would warm up by hitting six or seven practice balls and then rolling a few putts. Nevertheless, Jones won the United States Amateur Championship five times. He played in twenty-seven majors, winning thirteen of them. Bobby Jones is the only golfer in history to win all four majors in the same year. (5)

Few athletes have dominated a sport the way Jack Nicklaus dominated golf. Nicklaus believed he could win every tournament he played. So did his competitors. Jack's accomplishments include winning seventy-three professional tournaments. He finished in second or third place a combined ninety-four times. His record for winning majors is astonishing: six Masters, five PGA Championships, four U.S. Opens, and three British Opens. (9)

Bobby Jones and Jack Nicklaus were the two best golfers of the twentieth century. What made them so successful? Was it their physical skills? It's true that Jones and Nicklaus both had superior physical skills, but the same could be said for a lot of other players. So don't be fooled. What distinguished Bobby Jones and Jack Nicklaus was their ability to outplay the competition on the mental side of golf. When it came to mental skills, no one could match them.

Fundamentals

Every year, before the regular season begins, professional baseball teams head down to the warm-weather states for spring training. The athletes spend eight weeks working on the fundamentals of throwing, catching, and hitting. The same is true for professional football teams. In the dreaded heat of July and August, the players sequester themselves in training camp for two months and focus on the fundamentals of running, blocking, and tackling. Professional athletes are the best in the world at what they do. Nevertheless, every year, before the real games begin, they devote a significant amount of time to reviewing the fundamentals.

For every sport, the fundamentals are the most important skills. They are the building blocks of success. Nothing is more important.

Ben Hogan practiced and played golf almost every day. When he was too tired to swing his clubs, he would put them away and pull out a notebook. Hogan kept detailed records of the different aspects of his swing that he was working on. He also liked to watch other players while they practiced. If he saw something that might be helpful, he would make a note, reminding himself to try it out the next day. Hogan was especially interested in understanding the fundamentals of the golf swing, so he devoted the majority of his study time to this area. When he was convinced that he understood the fundamentals, he decided to write a book summarizing his findings. In typical fashion, Ben poured himself into the project. In the final analysis, he identified eight fundamentals. (4)

The purpose of this book is the same as Hogan's: to identify and give instruction on the fundamentals. However, the fundamentals discussed in this book are not concerned with the golf swing per se. Instead, they are the fundamentals for the mental side of golf. During the course of a twelve-year research project, I reviewed more than one thousand books and articles. A critical analysis of the information revealed six mental fundamentals for golf: playing with confidence, concentrating completely, managing nervousness, overcoming frustration, the pre-shot routine, and thinking straight.

Take the time to master the mental fundamentals and you'll outplay your competition just as Bobby Jones and Jack Nicklaus did.

PLAYING WITH CONFIDENCE

Confidence is everything in golf...it's confidence that makes a good player into a great player and eventually a champion.

—Fred Couples

Confidence means believing in your abilities. When you prepare to make a golf swing and you believe in your abilities, you're confident; raising the likelihood of making a successful shot. If you stand over the ball doubting your abilities, you obviously lack confidence; the chances of making a successful shot are now considerably lower.

If you have trouble maintaining your confidence on the golf course, take heart; you're in the company of two of the finest players in the world, Ben Hogan and Seve Ballesteros.

As an amateur player, and during the first part of his professional career, Ben Hogan was plagued by self-doubt. (4) Before his round began, he had no idea how he would play. Maybe he would shoot a 69, or maybe a 79. Hogan never knew. On his way to the first tee, he always felt unsure of himself. If he was playing well on one day, he would begin to worry about what might go wrong the next. According to Hogan, the doubting never stopped.

Seve Ballesteros is known all over the world for his self-assured style of play. But at the 1987 Masters, he lost his confidence. When regulation play ended, Ballesteros, Greg Norman, and Larry Mize were in a three-way tie for first place. It was Spain's greatest, versus Australia's greatest, versus the local favorite. This set the stage for a dramatic finish. Unfortunately, Ballesteros three-putted on the first hole of the play-off and was eliminated from the match. A look of disbelief swept over his face. On the next hole, with Norman in excellent position to par, Mize holed a 140-foot chip shot and won the Masters. The gallery exploded. Mize leaped into the air. Norman suffered a broken heart. As for Ballesteros, his confidence was deeply shaken.

Every golfer understands the importance of playing golf with confidence. Here are six strategies that will build confidence into your game: positive self-talk, play smart shots, replay good shots, minimize bad shots, play to your strengths, and build on your success.

Positive Self-Talk

During a round of golf, a player spends quite a bit of time talking to himself. These conversations seem subtle, but let me assure you they profoundly affect your confidence.

As you prepare to make a swing, keep your self-talk positive. If you tell yourself that you're sure of the distance, you have the right club in your hand, and you made a shot just like this one last week, you increase your confidence. On the other hand, if you tell yourself that the landing area is too small, there's water on the left, and the last time you played this hole you made a double bogie, you lower your confidence.

Greg Norman plays golf with great confidence. If you've ever seen him stride down a fairway or stalk a putt, you know what I'm talking about. Norman is a big believer in positive self-talk. Here's an example of how Greg talks to himself before a swing:

> You know this shot cold, you've knocked it stiff a thousand times, and now you're going to do it again.

And after a swing:

> Damn, Greg, I'm pretty impressed by that one. (10)

Negative self-talk is a sure way to lower your confidence. A case of the yips is a good example. The yips don't develop overnight. It takes time. Initially, it's not that the golfer misses a lot of short putts. It's that he keeps reminding himself, over and over, about the ones he did miss. The negative self-talk starts to lower his confidence and this causes him to miss a few more short putts. The misses are followed by more negative reminders, his confidence continues to fall, and he persists in missing short putts. The golfer isn't aware of it, but all of this negative self-talk accumulates in his brain. The longer these conversations go on, the more confidence he loses. Some of the best players in the world have turned themselves into nervous wrecks when they're within three feet of the cup, simply because of the way they talked to themselves.

When an alligator has a golf club in his hand, you would be amazed at how many positive things he says to himself. Alligators appreciate the power of positive self-talk, and you should, too.

Play Smart Shots

For humans, golf is a game of distance. Their number-one concern is how far they can hit the ball. To observe this phenomenon, go to a driving range during regular hours, and look down the row of golfers. It doesn't matter if they're holding a three-wood, a middle-iron, or a wedge; they are all trying to hit the ball as far as possible. Stop by a driving range during off hours, when the alligators practice and you'll observe a very different phenomenon. Gators swing their clubs smoothly. They're relaxed and unhurried. They're not concerned with distance. They're interested in playing smart shots, keeping the ball in the correct position.

Let's take a minute and follow a human and an alligator as they play a couple of holes. The first hole is a straight, 400-yard, par-four. John, the human, pulls out his driver and swings full speed. The ball travels 280 yards, but it's slightly off target and rolls into the rough. Charlie, the gator, hits a driver as well, but he swings smoothly. His target is 240 yards away. Everything goes as planned. For his approach shot, John will use a wedge. He makes good contact, but the tall grass wraps around the hosel and causes the club face to close slightly. As a result, the ball goes left, misses the green, and rolls into a bunker. Charlie selects a six-iron for his approach shot. He makes good contact; the club face stays square, and the ball lands on the green, 25 feet from the hole. John hits a sand wedge to within 8 feet of the hole and two-putts for a bogie. Charlie lags to 18 inches and taps in for a par.

The next hole is a medium length par-five that makes a sharp right turn at 415 yards. John crushes a drive down the center of the fairway, 285 yards out. Charlie hits a three-wood 220 yards down the left side of the fairway. John has 240 yards to the green. He pulls out his three-wood. He plans to cut the ball around the corner and land it on the green. He takes a mighty swing. Unfortunately, he over-cuts the shot just a bit, and the ball lands in the tall grass to the right of the green. Charlie decides to lay up to the 100-yard marker, his favorite distance into a green. He uses a five-wood and maintains proper rhythm. The ball lands in the fairway, 96 yards out. For his third shot, John decides to use a lob wedge. To his chagrin, the ball comes out of the grass too high and barely makes it onto the green. He is left with a 35-foot putt. Charlie selects a wedge for his third shot. He has a clean lie, so he's able to put the proper amount of spin on the ball. It lands on the green, checks up, and stops 12 feet from the hole. Both golfers two-putt and make par.

The final hole is a 159-yard par-three. The green slopes from back to front. John smashes an eight-iron, about 12 feet past the hole. Charlie hits an easy six-iron, about 7 feet below the hole. John's ball is out of position. His downhill putt slips past the hole and has to make a three-footer to save par. Charlie's ball is in the correct position, and he rolls it straight up the hill for a birdie.

John hits his shots considerably farther than Charlie. However, his ball tends to stray out of position, making his follow-up shots more difficult. After three holes, Charlie leads by two. He's playing smart shots, keeping his ball in the proper position, and feeling confident about his game.

Replay Good Shots

When you hit a really good shot—whether you're on the golf course or the practice tee—take a moment to dwell on what just happened. Recall, as vividly as you can, what the shot looked like, what it sounded like, and how it felt. In effect, what you're doing is developing a strong memory of the shot. A memory that you can replay in the future, anytime you wish.

Replaying good shots helped Ben Hogan overcome his problems with confidence. (4) Whenever he made a shot with which he was particularly happy, Hogan would replay it in his mind, over and over again. He would do so right after making the shot, later in the round, that evening in his hotel room, and throughout the following week. Each time Ben replayed the shot, he added confidence to his game.

Minimize Bad Shots

To play golf with confidence, you must know how to manage your successes and your failures. This strategy helps you minimize the negative effects of a bad shot.

Let's say you sliced an approach shot, missing the green by 30 feet. At this point, the last thing you want to do is spend extra time thinking about the shot. Unfortunately, that is exactly what many golfers do. They dwell on the failure. Without knowing it, they're lowering their confidence. Bad shots need to be minimized, the sooner the better. First, take a moment to identify what went wrong with the swing. Next, with the club still in your hand, address an imaginary ball and make the correct swing. In your mind, watch the ball take flight, soar through the air, and come to a stop exactly where you planned. Dwell on your success. By doing so, you're overriding the memory of a bad shot with the memory of a good one.

Play to Your Strengths

During the first two rounds of the 1999 PGA Championship, Hale Irwin, at fifty-four the oldest player in the field, was paired with Sergio Garcia, at nineteen the youngest. There was a big difference in their ages and in the strengths of their games. Irwin is one of the best iron players in the world, and he rarely three-putts. Garcia hits the ball a mile and has a deft touch around the green.

The course, Medinah Country Club, was set up to play over 7,400 yards. The par fives averaged 570 yards. For his second shot on the par fives, Irwin would lay up to his favorite yardage; he would hit a wedge into the green, and then either one-putt for birdie or two-putt for par. For his second shot, Garcia went to one of his strengths, the long ball. If he ended up in the rough or a greenside bunker, he would rely on his short game to get his third shot close. Both players took advantage of their strengths, played with confidence, and headed into the weekend with identical scores.

Playing to the strengths of your game will make you a more confident golfer. If you're hitting your driver well, use it more often, even on the shorter holes. If you're not hitting your driver well, leave it in the bag. You'll be hitting a longer second shot, but you'll feel more confident playing from the fairway instead of the rough. If you have a good short game and you're faced with a difficult long shot into the green, lay up to your favorite distance. From there you have a good chance of landing your approach shot on the green, oftentimes close to the hole. If you're a good sand player, instead of aiming for a safe part of the green, go for the pin. If things don't work out, you can still make par by getting up and down.

Build on Your Success

One of the statistics kept on the PGA Tour is driving accuracy: the percentage of times that the player's tee shot ends up in the fairway. The leaders in this category usually hit the fairway about 75 percent of the time.

Would you like to feel more confident with your driver? Here's a drill that will help. First, determine what percent of your drives find the fairway. Let's say it's 50 percent. Make it your goal to increase that percentage to 55. Spend some extra time on the practice tee. Focus your attention on hitting straighter, not longer, drives. Make this the number-one priority of your practice sessions. When you start hitting 55 percent of the fairways, you've reached your goal. Enjoy your success and the extra confidence that comes with it. Next, raise your goal to 60 percent. Continue to focus your practice sessions on hitting straight drives. With additional practice, you'll achieve your goal and feel even more confident off the tees. Now you're ready for 65 percent.

Would you like to be more confident with your putter? Try this drill. Place four balls 18 inches north of the cup. Keep putting the balls until you sink four in a row. Now move the balls 18 inches east of the cup. Keep putting until you sink four in a row from there. Do the same from south and west of the cup. Once you've come full circle, move the balls out three inches, and repeat the same procedure. Keeping in mind the importance of achieving success, gradually increase the distances by three inches. Soon you'll make more putts and feel more confident on the greens.

The first mental fundamental for golf is playing with confidence. As with all the mental fundamentals, you can learn this skill relatively quickly. It doesn't matter if you're a beginner or an accomplished player.

Chapter Summary

- Confidence means believing in your abilities.

- When you prepare to make a golf swing and you believe in your abilities, you're confident; raising the likelihood of making a successful shot.

- If you stand over the ball doubting your abilities, you obviously lack confidence; the chances of making a successful shot are now considerably lower.

- If you have trouble maintaining your confidence on the golf course, take heart; you're in the company of two of the finest players in the world, Ben Hogan and Seve Ballesteros.
- The following strategies will build confidence into your game: positive self-talk, play smart shots, replay good shots, minimize bad shots, play to your strengths, and build on your success.

CONCENTRATING COMPLETELY

I began to acquire my powers of concentration long ago when learning to create a variety of shots with only my old three-iron. I had to focus very intensely indeed on the grip, the setup, and the swing path to get the results I wanted out of that awkward, overlong club.

—Seve Ballesteros

From start to finish, the average golf swing takes less than two seconds. During that time, the club head travels approximately 25 feet. The average downswing lasts about two-fifths of a second. During that time, the club head accelerates to speeds in excess of 100 miles per hour. At impact, the angle of the club face has to be nearly perfect; the difference between a good shot and a bad shot is one-eighth of an inch. To make a successful swing, a player has to get all the right parts, in all the right places, at all the right times. Let your mind wander even a little bit, and something will probably go wrong.

My favorite story about a golfer's concentration involves Ben Hogan and Claude Harmon. The two were playing the twelfth hole at Augusta National. Harmon hit what looked to be a perfect shot. The ball landed on the green, rolled toward the hole, and dropped out of sight. Ace! Hogan, who seemed unaffected by what happened, finished the hole alone. As the two players were walking toward the next tee, Ben stopped for a moment to record the scores. "Claude," he asked, "what did you get there?" "I made a hole-in-one," said an incredulous Harmon. "Oh," said Hogan, as if he had not noticed. Now that's concentrating completely.

Concentration is the ability to focus your attention on the task at hand. Here are four strategies that will improve your ability to concentrate on the golf course: pick a target, focus on what's important, think about the process-not the outcome, and swing keys.

Pick a Target

When it comes to concentrating on the golf course, Raymond Floyd is one of the best. When Floyd takes his stance and settles into his swing, he concentrates so completely that his eyes seem to change color. As he prepares to make a swing, Raymond picks a specific target at which to aim the ball. Here's what happens next:

> I try to let all my senses take in as much about the target as I can, and as I go through my pre-shot routine, I narrow down to where, and on what path, I want to hit the ball. In my own case, once I get over the ball, I have a kind of rocking action with my feet that helps me filter that feel for the target through my body to my hands. When I feel at one with the target, that's when I pull the trigger. (3)

Having a target helps Raymond Floyd concentrate more effectively. Before teeing off, pick a specific target at which to aim the ball: a tree, a bush, or a brown spot in the fairway. For approach shots, instead of aiming for the middle of the green, aim at the flagstick, a small mound, or an undulation if one is visible. If you can't find an actual target, imagine a small, white circle, and aim for the center of it. As you prepare to putt, instead of aiming for the hole, aim for a blade of grass along the line, or a cluster of sand on the back of the cup. In each instance, you will be improving your concentration.

Focus on What's Important

Brad Faxon is one of the best putters on the PGA tour. When Faxon studies a putt, he places his thumbs on the sides of his head and his fingers at the end of his visor. It may look like he's shading his eyes from the sun, but what he's actually doing is blocking out the distractions around the green. Putting his hands in this position helps Brad focus on the important aspects of the putt: the surface of the green, the line he wants to take to the hole, and the speed he needs to get there. It also helps him block out what's not important: the other players, movements in the gallery, the scoreboard, etc.

Tiger Woods places his hands in a similar position for the same reason:

> A few years ago, I started cupping my hands around my eyes while I read putts. The reason I do it is not because I see more, it's because I see less. (19)

When you're preparing to make a tee shot, focus your attention on calculating the distance to your target, judging how the weather will affect the ball, choosing the right club, and making sure your self-talk is positive. These are the important aspects of the shot. When you're playing out of a bunker, concentrate on positioning your feet properly, opening the club face to the correct angle, deciding where you want the club head to enter the sand, and where you want to land the ball. Once again, these are the important aspects of the shot. In both cases, you will be concentrating more effectively.

Think about the Process-Not the Outcome

As you prepare to make a golf shot, you're likely thinking about one of two things: what you need to do to make the proper swing, or how the swing is going to turn out. In the first case, you're thinking about the process of the shot; in the second, you're thinking about the outcome.

Let's say your approach shot was long and ended up in a back-side bunker. It's a small green, and a pond guards the front. As you prepare to make your swing, you could think about planting your feet properly, getting your shoulders into the correct angle, putting the proper amount of spin on the ball, and determining the length of your follow-through. Alternately, you could think about catching too much sand and not getting the ball out of the bunker, or catching too little sand and hitting the ball into the water. In the first situation, you're thinking about the process of the shot, and this improves your concentration. In the second, you're thinking about the outcome, and this lowers your concentration.

As you prepare to make a putt, you have the same two options. You can focus your attention on the process of making the putt: keeping your head still, making a smooth takeaway, and accelerating through the ball. Or you can focus your attention on the outcome: leaving it short, pulling it left, or pushing it right. Focus your attention on the process, and I like your chances.

Swing Keys

A fellow golfer once asked Bobby Jones if he thought about anything just before starting his takeaway. Jones responded that he usually reminded himself of one or two things, and that if he did those things correctly, the shot was usually a success. (5) These players were discussing swing keys, a strategy that many accomplished golfers use to improve their concentration.

Here are some examples of swing keys: keep your left heel on the ground, start back slow, make a full shoulder turn, keep your head behind the ball, hit from the inside. Swing keys are last-second reminders. They're fresh in your memory, so your mind pays closer attention to them.

When it's time to make a golf swing, it's important that you turn up your concentration to the optimal level. In between swings, it's helpful to turn down your concentration. How far down is an individual matter.

Optimal Level

Seve Ballesteros is a strong-willed, emotional player who wears his feelings on his sleeve. Intensity is his middle name. Ballesteros likes to play aggressively and make things happen. His ability to concentrate under pressure has made him one of the best clutch players in the world. In between swings, Ballesteros turns his concentration down, but just a little. When he's on the golf course, Nick Faldo prefers to keep his thoughts and feelings in check. At times, he focuses so intently on his game that he appears unaware of anything else. Nick's personality is different than Seve's, but his concentration style is similar. In between swings, he turns his concentration down, just a bit. Fuzzy Zoeller has an easy-going personality. He likes to sing and whistle his way around the golf course. Zoeller is popular with the other players because he never takes himself too seriously and always has fun. In between swings, Fuzzy turns his concentration down noticeably. Lee Trevino, on the other hand, is an extrovert. When Trevino plays golf, he likes to talk to his caddy, the other players, the officials, the fans, to anyone who will listen. When he's swinging a club, Trevino concentrates at the optimal level. In between swings, it seems he's not concentrating at all.

Ballesteros, Faldo, Zoeller, and Trevino have each developed a style of concentration that fits their personality and their game. When it's time to make a shot, they turn up their concentration to the optimal level. In between swings, their level of concentration varies considerably. Their success provides strong evidence that one style is not superior to the others.

Turning up your concentration to the optimal level while making a swing and then turning it down to a preferred level in between swings takes some practice. Start with the style of concentration that you used during your best rounds, then make adjustments as necessary.

The ability to control your level of concentration will help you get into the cherished "zone." Getting into the zone is the ultimate exhilaration in golf. If you've ever been there, even for a short period of time, you know how exciting it can be. It was always a thrill for Sam Snead:

> Everything feels smooth. Your senses become sharper. You see all things more clearly. You can see the line of every putt. Your visualization is very clear. Your whole feel is different in the zone. Your touch seems different: its lighter, it's smoother, and it's easier. You're more relaxed. You don't think about anything but the shot you need to hit, and you think you can hit any shot you need to. (15)

Accomplished players reach the zone more often than average players, and they stay there for longer periods of time, sometimes for weeks. I believe that concentration is what gets a player into the zone. The more skilled you are at concentrating, the more time you'll spend there.

Chapter Summary

- Concentration is the ability to focus your attention on the task at hand.

- To make a successful golf swing you have to get all the right parts, in all the right places, at all the right times. Let your mind wander even a little bit, and something will probably go wrong.

- As you prepare to swing, turn up your concentration to the optimal level using these strategies: pick a target, focus on what's important, think about the process-not the result, and swing keys.

- Turn down your concentration in between shots. With a little experimentation, you can learn what level is best for you.

- The ability to concentrate gets a golfer into the zone and keeps him there.

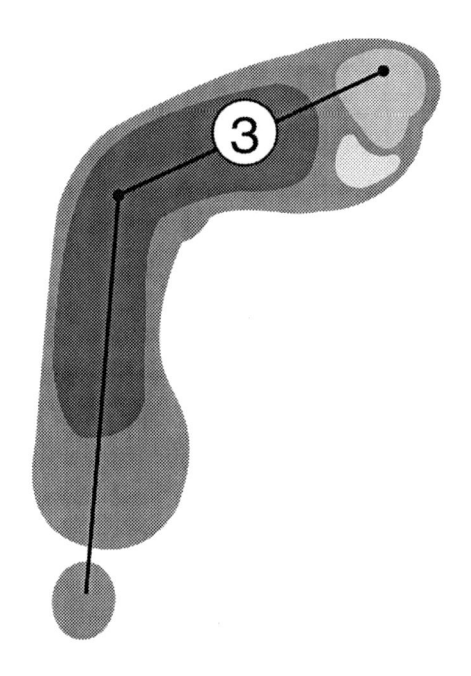

MANAGING NERVOUSNESS

If ever a man can learn to play each hole and each shot with a mind in which there is no fear of future or remembrance of past difficulties, his game will be as nearly unbeatable as it is possible to be.

—Bobby Jones

Golf is a nerve-wracking sport. In an article he wrote about his own nervousness, Bobby Jones revealed that on the morning of a big match he often felt sick to his stomach. Sometimes his hands would tremble so much he couldn't button his shirt collar. Once, as he prepared to make a shot that would determine the outcome of a match, his legs shook so badly that his knees started knocking together. (7)

You may find it hard to believe that someone of Jones's stature would become so nervous. After all, he is one of golf's most successful players. Jones knew what it took to win, and he had what it took. So you might be tempted to dismiss his words; perhaps he was overstating his case. He was a lawyer, you know. Let's learn a little more about nervousness and the golfer, and then you can draw your own conclusion.

What you and I call nervousness, scientists call the fight-or-flight response. Nervousness, or the fight-or-flight response if you prefer, was programmed into the brain centuries ago when wild animals ruled the earth. To survive, humans needed to be skilled at recognizing a potentially dangerous situation, such as a hungry lion, and then preparing themselves to fight or run to safety. If they were strong enough, or fast enough, they lived to see another day. If not, they became the lion's dinner.

Let's take a closer look at how the fight-or-flight response works. First, a person recognizes the potential for danger. Next, his brain sends a signal to the adrenal glands, which then release extra hormones into the bloodstream. Chemical and physiological reactions follow, quickly transforming the body to maximum size, strength, and speed. The extra hormones, which include adrenaline, circulate through the heart, causing it to beat faster. The increased pumping action delivers additional blood to the large muscles, which then expand and become more powerful. The hormones flow through the lungs, accelerating the breathing rate. This increases the amount of oxygen in the blood. Instead of regular fuel, the body now runs on a high-octane blend. The digestive system, not related to fighting or running, shuts down. This can result in a feeling of slight nausea. The blood that normally passes through the extremities is redirected to areas of the body associated with fighting or running. In turn, the hands and feet become cold. The dramatic increase in physiologic activity causes the body to overheat. To cool itself, the skin perspires. (8)

As you can see, the fight-or-flight response is a highly sophisticated reaction. However, it has a flaw, and therein lies the trouble for golfers: the response doesn't distinguish between a situation that is potentially dangerous physically and one that is potentially dangerous psychologically. During a round of golf, players do not encounter situations that threaten their physical well-being. However, they can find themselves in situations that threaten their psychological well-being. The possibility for intense frustration, loss of esteem, embarrassment, and failure, to name a few, await the player at any turn. These situations trigger a fight-or-flight response, making the golfer nervous.

The next time you're standing over an important shot and your heart starts beating a little faster, your muscles begin to tighten up, your breathing requires more effort, your stomach flip-flops, your hands and feet turn cold, and you start to perspire, you'll understand why. It happened to Bobby Jones, and it will happen to you.

Nervousness is a natural part of golf. At the competitive level, players experience nervousness all of the time. Many come to enjoy it. Nevertheless, it's important that you learn how to manage nervousness so it doesn't negatively affect your performance. Here are three effective remedies: distraction, deep breathing, and shake and stretch.

Distraction

When you're on the golf course and you start to feel nervous, you should first distract yourself. Whatever you're thinking about is triggering a fight-or-flight response. The sooner you stop thinking about it, the sooner you'll calm down.

I learned about the value of distraction while playing in my first competitive golf tournament. Walking up to the number-one tee, I felt jittery. The first player in my group hit a long, straight drive. The second player hooked his drive out of bounds. I started to think, "Oh no, what if that happens to me? What if I hook my drive out of bounds? That would be embarrassing. I would have to re-tee and then I'd be hitting my third shot." All I thought about was hooking my drive. The more I thought about it, the more nervous I became.

It was my turn to hit, and I was still thinking about hooking my drive out of bounds. Sure enough, I did. "What if I do it again," I immediately said to myself. "What if I hook my next shot out of bounds? That would be humiliating. I would have to re-tee, and then I'd be hitting my fifth shot." I continued to think about hooking my drive, and my nervousness intensified. Once again, I hooked it out of bounds. Thankfully, my third attempt found the fairway. It was a rough start, but I learned a valuable lesson: thinking about what makes you nervous makes you more nervous.

When your nerves start to jingle, distract yourself right away. Focus your attention on something else. Before the round begins, instead of standing around fidgeting, go to the practice tee and warm up. After that, head over to the practice green and focus all of your attention on judging the line and speed of your putts. If you still have some time, grab a scorecard and review your strategy for playing the course. If nervousness returns during your round, again, distract yourself right away. Focus your attention on course management, club selection, flight patterns, ball position, etc. Golfers have come up with all sorts of ways to distract themselves. A few examples include humming, singing, talking to themselves, talking with other players, telling jokes, enjoying the scenery, and thinking about a great shot they made in the past.

Deep Breathing

Breathing occurs so effortlessly, we rarely ever think about it. But did you know that breathing is a highly effective remedy for nervousness? When you start to feel nervous on the golf course, breathe deeply. Here's how:

- Inhale slowly through your nose, drawing the air into the abdominal area, then the lower chest area, and then the upper chest area.
- Continue inhaling until your lungs completely fill.
- Hold the air inside you for a count of three.
- Exhale slowly through your mouth.
- Repeat as necessary.

Shake and Stretch

At the completion of the third round of the 1986 British Open, Greg Norman held a one-stroke lead. Later that evening Norman was having dinner at a local restaurant and Jack Nicklaus stopped by his table. The Bear had a tip for The Shark. "The only thing you need to work on tomorrow is your grip," Jack said to Greg. "Check your grip pressure before every shot, and be sure you don't get too tight." (11)

When golfers become nervous, their muscles tighten up, disrupting the natural movements and rhythm of their swing. To restore normal flexibility, shake your hands and arms vigorously for a couple of seconds, then stretch your shoulders, back, and legs. This will loosen your muscles and restore normal flexibility. And remember, when you re-grip the club, "Be sure you don't get too tight."

Relaxing Off the Course

The following procedure is designed to put you in a state of deep physical and mental relaxation. You can use this procedure the night before an important round to help you stay calm and get a good night's sleep. You can also use it in the morning before you head over to the course:

Find a quiet room where you will not be interrupted. Sit in a comfortable chair and close your eyes. Do not lie down, as you might fall asleep. Place your feet flat on the floor with your hands comfortably on your thighs. Leave your arms and legs uncrossed. This position eliminates any physical sensations that might distract you.

Begin taking slow, deep breaths. Focus all of your attention on your breathing, nothing else. Let your mind go blank. Listen only to your breathing. When thoughts come in, simply let them pass through. If you are disrupted by something that requires your attention, take care of it and then resume the relaxation process.

As you continue breathing, begin to relax your body. Start with your feet and ankles. Relax these areas. Next, relax your lower legs and then your upper legs. Continue breathing slowly and deeply. Once the lower half of your body is completely relaxed, begin to focus on your back, shoulders, arms, hands. Relax each area as you go. Finally, relax your neck and face. As the muscles throughout your body ease, you may find that your head falls forward and that your upper body begins to droop a bit. If this position feels uncomfortable, slowly straighten yourself back up.

In about five to ten minutes, you will find yourself deeply relaxed, both physically and mentally. In this state, your mind is very receptive to suggestions. Now is the time to give yourself some positive suggestions. For example, "For the remainder of the evening, I'm going to feel calm and relaxed. When it's time to go to bed, I'll fall into a deep sleep. Tomorrow morning, I'll wake up feeling refreshed and energized. During the round, I will give every shot my complete concentration."

Remain in this state for as long as it feels comfortable. When you're ready, simply open your eyes and begin to focus your attention on some of the objects in the room.

Chapter Summary

- A fight-or-flight response occurs every time a person senses the potential for danger.

- Unfortunately, the response doesn't distinguish between a situation that is potentially dangerous physically and one that is potentially dangerous psychologically.

- During a round of golf, players can find themselves in situations that threaten their psychological well-being, triggering a fight-or-flight response and causing nervousness.

- Nervousness is a natural part of golf. To play your best, you have to manage it.

- Three effective remedies to manage nervousness include distraction, deep breathing, and shake and stretch.

- You can employ methods of physical and mental relaxation to curb nervousness the night before a big match or in the morning before you head over to the course.

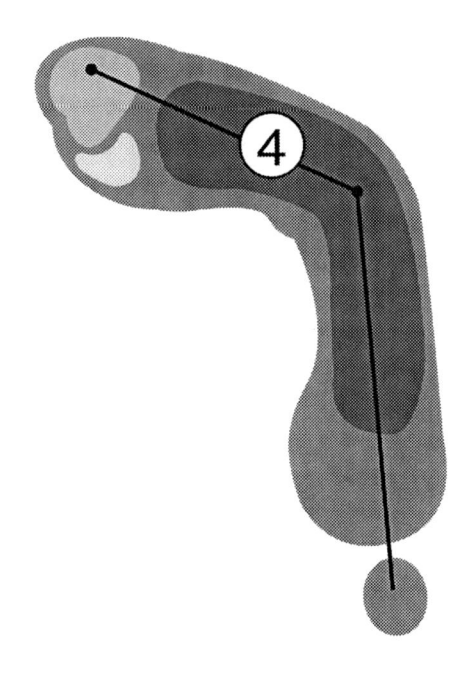

OVERCOMING FRUSTRATION

I always envy the man who can miss a shot and laugh about it—the fellow who takes neither himself nor his game too seriously. Surely that is golf seen in its true perspective...It would help most of us to enjoy the game if we would adopt that philosophy. But I confess with shame that I cannot do it. A bad shot, or some silly mistake at golf, makes me fairly boil inside.

—Bobby Jones

Another quality that makes alligators such good golfers is their patience. An alligator spends most of his day floating in a pond. As much as possible, he tries to not move or make a sound. With only his eyes and nostrils above water, he waits patiently for his prey to wander a little too close to the water. Sometimes he waits for hours, sometimes for days, and sometimes even longer. All of this waiting has taught the gator to be patient, a virtue that pays big dividends on the golf course.

Humans are not patient. Our lifestyle is fast-paced; we're always on the run and working against the clock. We look for ways to speed things up, not slow things down. The person who thinks and acts the quickest usually gets the reward. When things don't happen right away, we grow frustrated.

Golf is not a fast-paced sport. To be successful, a player has to be patient and wait for opportunities to present themselves. Sometimes it's a long wait. In golf, the tendency to become frustrated is a liability.

Anyone examining the shaft of Bobby Jones's putter would have learned that it was in less-than-perfect condition. Although he was fond of the club and remained loyal to it throughout his career, at times he felt that it betrayed him. On these occasions, Jones would have strong words with the putter and then slam it to the ground or launch it skyward. The shaft, which was made of hickory wood, was often damaged during the outbursts. After a cooling-off period, Jones would make the necessary repairs to the club, thereby renewing the friendship. Bobby Jones was a competitor. He always wanted to play his best. When he didn't, he felt frustrated. Once, while playing the British Open at St. Andrews, he became so frustrated that he walked off the course in the middle of a round.

As an amateur player, Curtis Strange, after making a bad shot or posting a high score, would act out his frustration for everyone to see. By his own admission he was a "hothead." (17) To realize his full potential as a professional player, Curtis needed to learn how to manage his anger. Fortunately, he did. In 1988, he was named PGA Player of the Year. The following year he became the first player since Ben Hogan to win consecutive United States Open Championships. At this point in his career, many people considered Curtis Strange the best golfer in the world.

It's not just tour players competing for big prize money who encounter frustration. The weekend golfer also experiences his fair share. You can play one of the best rounds of your life on one day and one of the worst rounds the next. You can have a great front nine and a terrible back nine. You can go birdie, par, birdie, and then double bogie, bogie, double bogie. You can play well, but score poorly. You can play poorly, but score well. You can love and hate golf at the same time!

If you play golf, frustration is no stranger. Sooner or later your performance doesn't measure up to your expectations, and you start to "boil inside." But to play your best, you have to overcome frustration. Sam Snead agrees:

> I'm not saying that I haven't helicoptered a club or two—nearly all great players have at one time or another. But not until they got control of their emotions did they really mature as players. (15)

Of all the emotions that a round of golf can stir up, frustration can be the most difficult to manage. For starters, players are expected to handle their frustration quietly. Outward displays of aggravation are not welcomed. As the equipment used to televise golf tournaments improves, players have been heard uttering all sorts of profanities that are broadcast around the world. This behavior usually results in a firm reprimand.

Some players try to manage their frustration by holding it inside. They've seen frustrated golfers act like buffoons, and they have no interest in following that example. However, when you try to hold too much frustration inside, you begin to work against the strong physiological tendencies programmed to release it. Holding too much frustration inside is like holding a beach ball underwater: you can do it for a while, but sooner or later you'll lose control.

Bobby Jones stormed off the course at St. Andrews because he could no longer manage his frustration. He allowed too much of it to build up inside him, and eventually he lost control. Jones deeply regretted his actions and promised never to repeat them. Had he released his frustration before it reached such a high level, he could have avoided the embarrassing situation entirely. The key to overcoming frustration is releasing it along the way before too much builds up. Here are three strategies for releasing frustration: talk it out, use your imagination, and mental time-outs.

Talk It Out

You can release your frustration by holding a conversation with yourself. First, identify exactly what you're thinking and feeling. Next, put your thoughts and feelings into words. For example, "I'm really frustrated right now. That was a terrible swing. What was I thinking? I feel very angry." Or you might say, "I can't believe how poorly things are going right now. I can play so much better than this. This is so frustrating. I should have never played that shot. That was such an impulsive decision. I feel really upset right now."

When you're talking out frustration, give yourself some leeway. If it's necessary to turn up the volume, go ahead. No one is listening but you. But as you talk out the frustration, be sure not to direct it at yourself. When golfers direct frustration at themselves, the situation usually worsens. Instead, tell the driver how badly it performed. Let the wedge know that if it doesn't shape up, it's going back in the garage. Inform the ball that it has one more chance or it's going to the bottom of the lake.

Use Your Imagination

You can use your imagination to release frustration. The mind and body are so closely linked that imagining yourself doing something has nearly the same effect as actually doing it.

Let's say you pulled a tee shot into the trees, and instead of punching out to the fairway you decide to go for the green. You make good contact with the ball, but it hits a tree branch and drops straight down. Now you're frustrated. You're in a little better position, so you decide to go for the green a second time. Once again, the ball hits a tree branch. Now you're really frustrated. What thoughts are you having? What do you feel like doing? Maybe you're thinking about swinging the club like a baseball bat. Perhaps you feel like hammering the ground with it. Go ahead! Imagine yourself taking a swing. Imagine yourself hammering the ground. Your goal is to release the frustration, and it's important that you're successful.

Let's say you played an especially poor round, and on the final hole you sliced your approach shot into the water. This is your fifth water ball of the day. At this point, you're ready to explode. Your overriding impulse is to throw your golf bag into the middle of the lake. You've reached a high level of frustration; ideally, you would have released some of it before now. Unfortunately, you haven't. But rather than actually throwing the bag, imagine throwing it instead.

When you use your imagination to release frustration, be as vivid as possible. The more closely your imaginary experience resembles the real experience, the more frustration you will release.

Mental Time-Outs

If a football player jumps offside, the coach can send in a substitute. The player comes off the field, takes a seat on the bench, and has plenty of time to think about what he did wrong and how to correct it. Should a baseball pitcher give up two walks and then a home run, the manager can stop the game, walk out to the mound, and help his pitcher regain his composure. If that doesn't help, he can change pitchers. When the momentum shifts in a basketball game, one of the players can signal for a time-out. The entire team comes off the court and talks with the coaching staff about what adjustments they need to make.

There are no time-outs in golf. Players are not allowed to leave the course to talk things over with their coach. Substituting one golfer for another is obviously out of the question. Between shots, however, golfers have time to take mental time-outs.

Taking a mental time-out allows you to get your mind off whatever has caused your frustration. When you take a mental time-out, you can go wherever you want and do whatever you want. Go home and relax in your favorite chair. Hop in your boat and go fishing. If you run into a long wait on a par three, instead of fuming at the group in front of you, take a mental time-out and ski down a snow-covered mountain. The possibilities are endless.

When you stop thinking about what's frustrating you and start to think about something you enjoy, you begin to relax. When it's time for your next shot, you'll feel calmer.

Expectations

Expectations are powerful things, and golfers need to be careful with them. Unrealistic expectations create unnecessary frustration. When you're on a golf course, be sure to match your expectations with your level of skill.

If hitting an approach shot onto a green means carrying the ball over a creek that is 200 yards away, it may be better to lay up. If you're hitting your driver inconsistently, try using a three-wood off the tees. If the pin is in a difficult position, maybe it's not the best target. Besides, you'll feel calmer walking up to the green with a putter in your hand instead of a sand wedge. You can hit a perfect tee shot only to have a gust of wind push the ball into a fairway bunker. That's frustrating. An approach shot that's rolling toward the green can take a bad hop and end up in a bunker. That's irritating. Your putt, which was on line and had the right amount of speed, can hit a spike mark and be thrown off course. That will drive you crazy.

Keep in mind that you have only partial control over what happens on a golf course. Maintaining this perspective makes it easier to overcome frustration.

It Takes a Lifetime to Learn

Ben Hogan started playing golf at an early age. As a kid, he would use the front lawns in his neighborhood as the greens. When he was a little older, Hogan took a job as a caddy at the Glen Garden Club in Fort Worth, Texas. It was here that he began to study the game in earnest. After much observation, Ben decided that a member named Ed Stewart had the best swing, so he modeled his swing after Stewart's. He decided that the club's pro, Ted Longworth, had the best grip, so he fashioned his grip after Longworth's. It wasn't too much longer until Hogan decided that golf would be his life's work.

When he was nineteen years old, Gary Player qualified for the British Open. He went on to compete in this tournament for forty-five consecutive years. Player is one of only five golfers, along with Gene Sarazen, Ben Hogan, Jack Nicklaus, and Tiger Woods, to win all four professional majors. Gary is one of golf's most victorious players. At this point in his career, he would like to become the first golfer in history to win a professional tournament in six different decades. He is convinced that if he continues to work on his game, he will achieve his goal.

A television interviewer asked Byron Nelson, who was eighty-four years old at the time, how his game was going. Nelson took the question seriously and went on for several minutes, explaining in great detail several aspects of his swing that he was trying to improve. Byron had a legendary career. His accomplishments include winning eleven straight professional tournaments and making the cut in 113 consecutive tries. At the age of eighty-four, you might think that Nelson would be resting on his laurels. But he wasn't. He was still looking for ways to improve his game.

Ben Hogan, Gary Player, and Byron Nelson have taught us an important lesson about golf: it takes a lifetime to learn. When things aren't going your way, and you're discouraged, remind yourself about this lesson.

Chapter Summary

- Every golfer experiences frustration. Sooner or later, your performance doesn't measure up and you start to boil inside.

- When you're on the golf course and frustration starts to build, it's important to release it before it reaches an unmanageable level.

- Three proven strategies for releasing frustration are: talk it out, use your imagination, and mental time-outs.

- When managing frustration, always be respectful to yourself, to the other players, and to the course.

- Unrealistic expectations create unnecessary frustration. Be sure to match your expectations with your level of skill.

- When you're feeling discouraged, remind yourself of the lesson taught by Ben Hogan, Gary Player, and Byron Nelson: it takes a lifetime to learn.

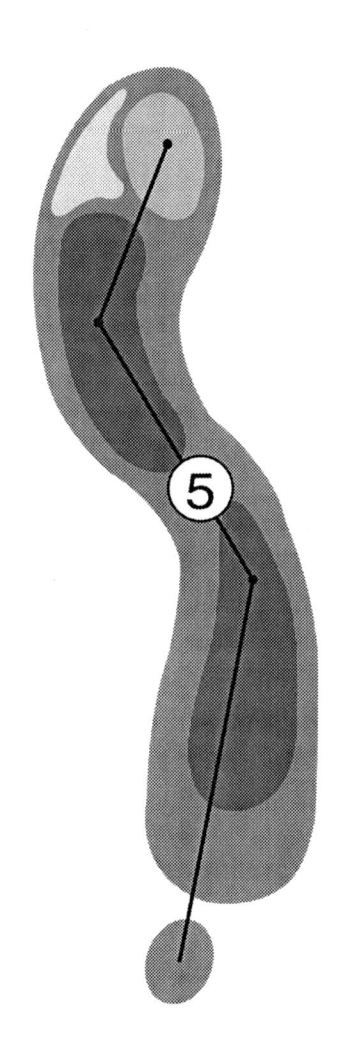

THE PRE-SHOT ROUTINE

Most good golfers use precisely the same routine for every shot they play.

—Tom Watson

Tom Watson observed that good players use the same routine for every shot they play. The same could be said about Watson. If you watch film of Tom preparing to make a shot early in his career, during his heyday on the PGA Tour, and now on the Champions Tour, you will see that very little has changed. The amount of time he spends on his pre-shot routine, the procedures he follows, and his unique mannerisms are all remarkably similar. The golf world waited a long time for someone to come along who could beat Jack Nicklaus. Watson was that player. In part, Watson's success was due to how well he prepared himself to make good golf shots.

To play your best, you have to know how to prepare yourself to make good shots. These preparations, collectively known as the pre-shot routine, are based on a simple principle: when you give your mind exact instructions about what you want to do, success is more certain. For teaching purposes, we will discuss the pre-shot routine as a three-step procedure. In Step One, you assess the variables of the shot. In Step Two, you decide on the shot you want to play. In Step Three, you prepare yourself to make the shot.

Step One: Assess the Variables of the Shot

For every shot in golf, the player should consider a number of variables. In particular, you need to calculate certain distances, examine the lie, and determine how the weather will affect the ball.

While preparing to make a tee shot, you need to calculate the distance to the preferred landing area. For par-three holes, the landing area is usually somewhere on the green. Par-four and par-five holes are designed for either a long drive or one that is strategically placed. If the hole calls for a long drive, and you normally carry your drive 230 yards, then the landing area is that distance. If the hole requires a strategically placed drive, you need to calculate the distance to that specific area of the fairway. Usually, the scorecard contains distances that will assist you. If not, you need to make your best estimate.

As you prepare to make an approach shot, knowing several distances will be helpful. First, calculate the distance to the center of the green. Typically, yardage markers are placed throughout the fairway to help you determine the distance. Once you have this number, it's simply a matter of adding or subtracting yards to determine other distances you may want to know: to the front of the green, to the pin, and to your target.

Examine the lie in order to determine how it will affect the flight pattern of the ball. If you're a right-handed player and the ball is above your feet, the ball will typically move from right to left. The farther the ball is above your feet, the more it will curve. If the ball is below your feet, the flight pattern will be from left to right. Again, the farther the ball is below your feet, the more it will turn. For left-handed players, the flight patterns will be the opposite.

If you have an uphill or downhill lie, you'll need to adjust your club selection, posture, and ball position accordingly.

If the ball is in the fairway, you can anticipate a normal amount of backspin and roll. If you're hitting out of the rough, a certain amount of grass will get pinched between the ball and the club face at impact. The more grass, the less distance the ball will travel in the air. Also, the more grass, the less backspin on the ball, which means that it will roll farther after it lands.

When determining how the weather will affect the ball, you need to consider wind, moisture, temperature, and altitude.

Generally, the wind moves in one direction. However the wind will swirl around obstacles in its path, such as trees or hills. Tossing some grass clippings into the air will usually give you an accurate read on the direction and strength of the wind. If you suspect that it's moving in several directions, check the flag, the tops of trees, and the surface of any nearby water for additional information.

Moisture increases the density of the air, which means that the ball encounters more resistance during its flight. The higher the moisture level, the shorter the distance the ball travels.

Golf balls are manufactured to perform their best in moderate to warm temperatures. When it's cold, the ball becomes harder, is less responsive, and therefore flies a shorter distance. When you play in cold weather, it's a good idea to hold the ball in your hand or keep it in a pocket whenever possible. You may also want to consider changing to a softer ball.

The higher the altitude, the thinner the air, which means the ball encounters less resistance during its flight. As a result, it travels farther. In mountainous areas, the distance that you normally hit each of your clubs increases significantly.

Step Two: Decide on the Shot You Want to Play

Having assessed the variables, you're now prepared to decide on the shot you want to play. Keep in mind the principle on which the pre-shot routine is based: when you give your mind exact instructions about what you want to do, success is more certain.

When preparing to make a tee shot, instead of saying "I'm going to rip this drive a mile," it's more helpful to say, "I'm going to make a full shoulder turn, accelerate the club head through the ball, and play a slight draw." These are exact instructions. Your mind knows precisely what you want to do. The chances of making a successful shot are now higher. When preparing for an approach shot, if you normally say "I'm going to hit a seven-iron. I'm pretty sure that's the right club," it's better to say, "I'm going to hit a medium seven-iron, play a slight fade, and land the ball just below the hole." The instructions are exact, your mind knows what you want to do, and the likelihood of success is higher. As you prepare to make a long putt, instead of saying, "I'm going to roll the ball up there and try to get it close to the hole," try saying, "I'm going to lag the ball to within two feet of the hole and leave myself an uphill putt for par." Once again, the chances of success are higher.

Step Three: Prepare Yourself to Make the Shot

Steps One and Two of the pre-shot routine are standard for all golfers. Step Three allows for personal preferences and variations. Here are four procedures that will prepare you to make successful shots: visualization, feeling the swing, hearing the shot, and recalling a similar shot. When developing a pre-shot routine, be sure to experiment with all of these procedures, singularly and in different combinations. Feel free to add your own personal touches wherever helpful. Once you've developed an effective routine, make it a habit. Use it for every shot you play. You should carefully consider any changes on the practice tee before implementing them on the course.

In order to visualize, stand away from the ball and, in your mind, watch yourself making a successful shot. Your setup is correct. Your swing is smooth. The flight pattern of the ball is perfect. And the ball lands in the middle of your target. When you visualize a shot, everything goes according to plan.

Greg Norman uses visualization as part of his pre-shot routine. (11) First, he sees the ball as it leaves the club face and starts on its way up. Second, he sees the apex of the flight pattern as a dark, circular opening in the sky. Third, he watches as the ball lands, rolls, and comes to a stop. Jack Nicklaus also uses visualization. (9) To begin, he sees the ball resting at the target, as if he has already finished the shot. Next, he sees the flight pattern the ball will take on its way to the target. Finally, he watches as he takes his stance and makes the perfect swing. Norman prefers to visualize his shots in the proper sequence. Nicklaus visualizes his shots in reverse order. Their personal preferences are different, but their objective is the same: they want to give their mind exact instructions on how to make the shot.

Bobby Jones found visualization especially helpful on the green:

> I can truthfully say that I have holed very few putts when I could not definitely see the path that the ball should follow into the hole. The line sometimes seems as clear as if someone marked it out in paint. (6)

Another helpful procedure involves focusing your attention on the feel of the swing you want to make. The more familiar you are with how the movements of the swing should feel, the more likely it is that you will replicate those movements during the actual swing.

There are two popular variations to this procedure. In the first, you stand away from the ball and, in your mind, feel yourself making the perfect swing. You swing an imaginary club at an imaginary ball. In the second variation, you address an imaginary ball, but you swing the club that you are going to use during the actual shot. Again, it's a matter of personal preference.

In order to hear the shot, you stand away from the ball and imagine the sounds associated with the shot you want to make. Listen for the "whoosh" as the club makes its way toward the ball. Hear the "click" as the club head strikes the ball. Notice the "sizzle" as the ball takes flight. If it's a bunker shot, recognize the "thump" as the club head enters the sand. When it's time to make the actual shot, your mind will use the sounds to help guide your swing.

In addition to using visualization in his pre-shot routine, Greg Norman also recalls a similar shot that he made successfully in the past:

> If on a certain occasion in my career I was able to slam a one-iron two hundred and sixty yards over water to within a foot of the flag, I have a strong and pleasant mental record of that shot, and when I come to a similar situation, it's natural to call on that memory. (11)

As you recall a similar successful shot you made, pay close attention to the way the shot looks, feels, and sounds. The memory, now fresh in your mind, will serve as a map for the shot at hand.

When he's preparing to make a putt, Arnold Palmer uses visualization, feeling the swing, and hearing the shot. First, he imagines what the putter will feel like in his hands while he makes the actual stroke. Next, he listens for the sound of the putter as it strikes the ball. Finally, he watches as the ball rolls along the line, takes the break, and drops into the cup. (12)

Every alligator I know uses a pre-shot routine. They understand how important it is to the quality and consistency of their game. If a pre-shot routine is not part of your game, now is the time to add one.

The following examples offer a quick review of the pre-shot routine.

Example One

You're preparing to hit a tee shot on a straight, 390-yard, par-four hole. You normally hit your driver 260 yards, but there are several fairway bunkers at that distance. In your estimation, the fairway begins to narrow considerably at 240 yards. You determine that the ball will roll 10 yards after it lands. Next, you toss some grass clippings into the air and check the tops of the trees near the green. A steady wind blows from right to left. You estimate that it will move your ball 10 yards to the left. No other weather conditions come into play.

You've assessed the variables, and now you're ready to decide on the shot you will play. After careful consideration, you decide to play a 230-yard tee shot, which means you will use a three-wood. You will play a straight shot and let the wind push the ball left. Factoring in 10 yards of roll and 10 yards of right-to-left movement while the ball is in the air, the target area is 220 yards from the tee, 10 yards to the right of the center of the fairway.

Example Two

You're getting ready to play an approach shot from out of the rough. The green is medium-sized and relatively flat. You locate the 100-yard marker and determine that the center of the green is 90 yards away. The flagstick is back-left, so you add seven yards. The distance to the pin is 97 yards. You want to be sure that your shot lands on the green; you estimate the distance to the front of the green at 80 yards. You have a flat lie, but the ball rests in some tall grass. This means less backspin and more roll. Given the length of the rough, you estimate that the ball will roll 11 yards after it lands. The air contains a considerable amount of moisture, and a stiff wind blows directly into your face. You determine that the weather conditions lengthen the shot by 15 yards.

Now it's time to decide on the shot you will play. When making an approach shot, the key is to decide where you want to land the ball. Given the variables of this shot, some additional calculations are necessary. The pin is 97 yards away. You expect the ball to roll 11 yards after it hits. You subtract 11 from 97. The distance to the target area is 86 yards. Add 15 yards because of the weather, and you need to hit a straight, 101-yard shot, perfect for your sand wedge.

Preparing Yourself before the Round

So far, we've discussed procedures you can use on the course to prepare yourself to make good golf shots. Now we will look at a procedure that prepares you to play well before your round begins.

Sam Snead used this procedure throughout his career. I'll let him explain it to you:

> Whenever I had an important round to play the following day, I would set aside some quiet time the night before to think about what lay ahead. I'd find a comfortable chair in a quiet room and just sit there with my eyes closed, imagining the round I faced. I'd begin on the first tee, visualizing the hole and actually seeing myself

play my tee shot, second shot and so on. Naturally, I'd see only good things happening because you must do everything you can to put yourself in a positive frame of mind. (16)

When he walked up to the first tee the following morning, Snead knew exactly how he wanted to play every shot on every hole. Now that's being prepared!

Chapter Summary

- To play your best you have to know how to prepare yourself to make good golf shots. These preparations are collectively known as the pre-shot routine.

- The pre-shot routine is as follows. In Step One, you assess the variables of the shot. In Step Two, you decide on the shot you want to play. In Step Three, you prepare yourself to make the shot.

- Procedures such as visualization, feeling the swing, hearing the shot, and recalling a similar shot can help with Step Three of the pre-shot routine.

- Almost all accomplished players have a pre-shot routine. They understand how important it is to the quality and consistency of their game. If you do not have a pre-shot routine, now is the time to add one.

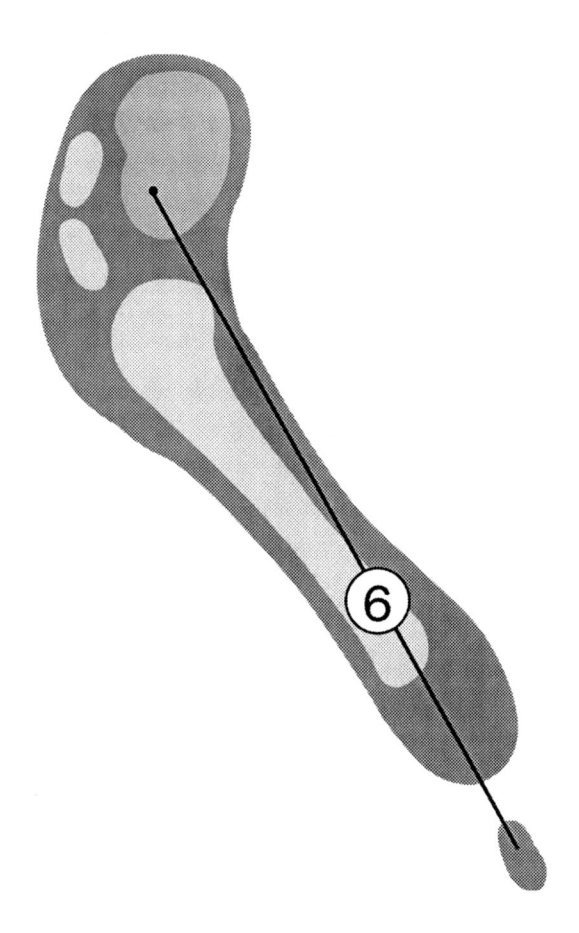

THINKING STRAIGHT

You must understand that it is your mind that will have the most to do with how you play in the big match.

—Harvey Penick

A comparison between the alligator brain and the human brain would reveal several significant differences. Most noticeable is that the alligator brain is smaller than the human brain. Another difference is the number of parts. Comparatively, the alligator brain has fewer parts. Also noteworthy is the manner in which the two brains think. Because their brains are smaller and have fewer parts, alligators tend think more simply.

When it comes to solving mathematical equations and explaining scientific phenomena, the human brain, with its complex thinking ability, wins out. However, on the golf course the alligator brain proves superior. The reason is that when alligators think, they stay with the basics and never complicate things unnecessarily. Humans, on the other hand, tend to over analyze, often making mountains out of molehills. This is particularly true when they have a golf club in their hand. In a sport that places a premium on keeping things simple and thinking clearly, the advantage goes to the alligator every time. You might think that its small brain would disadvantage the alligator, but on the golf course it's one more reason why alligators make good golfers.

Cognitive Psychology

For quite a long time, psychologists believed that a person's feelings determined his thoughts. For example, a person would begin to feel sad and this feeling would cause him to have certain thoughts, such as, "Things are not going very well for me right now. Maybe I deserve to feel bad. I'll probably feel this way for a long time. There isn't anything I can do about it." Because a person's feelings were considered to be so influential, very often a psychologist's first question would be, "How are you feeling?"

Then along came the cognitive psychologists who believe the opposite. Cognitive psychologists believe that a person's thoughts determine his feelings. In other words, a person first has the thoughts, "Things are not going very well for me right now. Maybe I deserve to feel bad. I'll probably feel this way for a long time. There isn't anything I can do about it." These thoughts cause him to feel sad.

The psychologists who believed that feelings determine thoughts based their belief on theoretical notions. Cognitive psychologists did not make this mistake. They based their belief on scientific evidence. For the past twenty-five years, in research laboratories around the world, cognitive psychologists have empirically demonstrated that thoughts determine feelings. Their findings have revolutionized psychology. Now, instead of asking people how they feel, many psychologists ask them "What are you thinking?

Cognitive psychologists have also discovered that the human brain uses thinking patterns to process information. Thinking patterns help the person process information accurately, in other words, to think straight. That's the good news. The bad news is that on occasion, the complex nature of the brain causes the development of a faulty thinking pattern. When this happens the brain does not process information correctly. The person's thoughts become distorted. In effect, they stop thinking straight. Let's head over to the golf course to see how faulty thinking patterns affect the golfer.

As we discussed earlier, golf places a premium on keeping things simple and thinking clearly. When you're on the golf course and a faulty thinking pattern develops inside your head, it can spell big trouble. Your brain begins to process information inaccurately. Instead of keeping things simple, things become complicated. Instead of thinking clearly, your thoughts become distorted. Additionally, because thoughts determine feelings, you can no longer trust what you feel. In this frame of mind a golfer's performance naturally declines. The information inside his head is incorrect. He begins to draw the wrong conclusions and make poor decisions. Instead of playing thoughtfully, he plays impulsively. Confidence and concentration fall off. Nervousness and frustration take over. The longer the faulty thinking pattern remains, the more distorted his thoughts become.

When a golfer's performance declines for a time, he usually assumes that something is wrong on the physical side of his game. The goal is to identify the problem and then make the necessary corrections. To that end, he begins to spend more time on the practice tee. Perhaps he calls his instructor to schedule a few lessons. Sometimes these efforts help and sometimes they do not. If he is unsuccessful at fixing the problem, golf becomes a very unpleasant sport. If the problem persists, he could be headed for a slump.

Perhaps the decline has nothing to do with the physical side of his game. Maybe, the reason for the poor performance is mental. Many times, when you're not hitting it straight, it's because you're not thinking straight.

Let's check in with the cognitive psychologists to see if they can help a golfer who has developed a faulty thinking pattern. Fortunately, the answer is yes. Cognitive psychologists are experts at helping people keep their thinking on track so that their feelings stay on track. They have developed a simple, effective, two-step procedure for doing so. In Step One you identify the faulty thinking pattern. In Step Two you replace the distorted thoughts. In the remainder of this chapter we will take a close look at this valuable procedure.

Step One: Identify the Faulty Thinking Pattern

Golfers need to watch for six faulty thinking patterns: self-criticism, binocular thinking, thinking in the future or the past, perfectionism, labeling, and thinking about what you don't want to do. If you're like most players, only two or three of the faulty patterns affect your game. Once you're familiar with those patterns, identifying them is a simple matter.

Self-Criticism

When you're not playing well, it's important to evaluate your game, not your personality. But when you're busy criticizing yourself, you lose this important distinction. Instead of looking for flaws in your swing, you look for flaws in your character.

Here are some examples: "I can't believe how pathetic I am." "What a loser." "I'm such a terrible player." "How can I be such a moron?" "What's wrong with me?"

Golfers who are involved in self-criticism become so preoccupied with finding problems in their personality that they don't take the time to correct the problem in their swing. As a result, they continue to play poorly, which results in more self-criticism, which causes them to play even more poorly.

Binocular Thinking

When you look through a pair of binoculars, things that are far away appear to be close. When you turn the binoculars around and look through the other end, things that are close appear to be far away. Depending on how you use them, binoculars can either magnify or minimize. When golfers are thinking straight, they use their binoculars to magnify their accomplishments and minimize their disappointments. However, when this faulty thinking pattern gets in their head, they do the opposite. They diminish their successes and highlight their failures.

Here are some examples of how to use your binoculars properly when you're on the golf course. You hit an extra-long drive and replay the shot in your head several times as you walk down the fairway. You finish a round in which you hit thirteen of the eighteen greens, and remind yourself that hitting approach shots is one of the strengths of your game.

Here are some examples of how not to use your binoculars. You miss a short putt and obsess about it for five minutes. Instead of checking up, your ball rolls through the green and into a back-side bunker. You recall similar shots from the past that did not hold the green, and then tell yourself that you've never had a good short game.

Using your binoculars properly builds confidence. When you use them improperly, the opposite occurs.

Thinking in the Future or the Past

Thinking in the future or the past is the one of the most common faulty thinking patterns for golfers. Be on the lookout for this one.

When you're deciding what club to hit into the fifth green, but you're thinking about the water along the sixth fairway, you've allowed your thoughts to wander into the future. If you're preparing to hit your tee shot on the seventh hole, and you're predicting what your score might be on the front nine, you're thinking in the future. When you're lining up a putt on the fourteenth green, and you're reminiscing about the sand save you made on eleven, you're thinking in the past. If you're deciding whether to lay up or go for the green on eighteen, but you're reviewing the details from a business meeting you had earlier in the day, your thoughts have drifted into the past.

Here's the problem. When you're thinking in the future or the past, you're not focusing all of your attention in the present, on the shot at hand. As a result, your concentration falls, and so do the chances of making a successful shot.

Perfectionism

Very few players have ever hit a golf ball as consistently as Ben Hogan. In his mind, Hogan had a specific trajectory, flight pattern, and distance for every shot he played. It seems to me that most of his shots went just as he planned. Nevertheless, according to Hogan, only one or two shots per round went as he intended. (4) Hogan was a perfectionist.

Here are some illustrations of perfectionism:

> Your tee shot on a dogleg right is straight and lands on the right side of the fairway. You're left with a clear shot to the green with only a seven-iron. Even so, you're disappointed. You wanted to fade the ball around the corner and then wedge it into the green. You conclude that it was a bad shot.

> You roll a 50-foot putt 7 feet past the hole. As you walk up to mark the ball, you comment to your playing partner, "Have you ever seen a worse putt?"

Thinking like a perfectionist puts unnecessary pressure on a golfer. Sooner or later, your nerves start to jangle. Toward the end of his career, Ben Hogan developed great difficulty making short putts. I think the reason is that all the pressure from the perfectionism caught up with him.

Labeling

When a person is labeled, it influences the way others treat him. For example, if a student is given the label "motivated," it's very likely that his teachers will spend more time with him, offer more encouragement, and reward him with higher grades. On the other hand, if a student is labeled "problematic," his teachers will tend to keep a distance, provide more negative feedback, and give him lower grades.

When a person is labeled, he has a tendency to behave in ways that are consistent with the label. To illustrate, a person who is given the label "artistic" will begin to spend more time in creative endeavors. A person who is labeled "lazy" will start to spend more time on the couch. When a golfer is given a positive label, it's helpful. When the label is negative, it's harmful. For example, when a golfer is given the label "accurate driver," he will begin to hit more fairways. A player who decides that he's a "weak putter" will start to miss more putts.

When you find yourself thinking in terms of labels, be careful. If the label is constructive, accept it. If it's negative, reject it immediately.

Thinking About What You Don't Want to Do

During a round of golf, have you ever found yourself thinking in terms of what you don't want to do, instead of what you want to do? For example, you're preparing to hit a tee shot. Right before you take your stance, you say to yourself, "Don't hit it left into the lake." Or perhaps you're getting ready to play a bunker shot. As you sink your feet into the sand, you give yourself a reminder, "Don't hit this thin."

Thinking about what you don't want to do causes confusion. What does "Don't hit it left" mean? Hit it straight? Hit it right? Play a fade? Your mind doesn't know what shot you want to play. To end the uncertainty, your brain disregards the "don't." "Don't hit it left into the lake" becomes "Hit it left into the lake." "Don't hit this thin" translates to "Hit this thin." When you're on a golf course, always think in terms of what you want to do. This eliminates confusion, keeps things simple, and promotes clear thinking.

Let's review the six faulty thinking patterns. Keep an eye out for the ones that affect your game:

Self-Criticism: You're not playing well. Instead of looking for the problem in your swing, you're looking for the problem in your personality.

Binocular Thinking: You magnify your failures and minimize your accomplishments. You miss every opportunity to build up your confidence, and take advantage of every opportunity to tear it down.

Thinking in the Future or the Past: Instead of focusing your attention in the present, on the shot at hand, you allow your thoughts to wander into the future or the past. This divides your attention and lowers your concentration.

Perfectionism: Thinking like a perfectionist creates unrealistic expectations and unnecessary pressure. Eventually, your nerves start to jangle, and your performance drops off.

Labeling: You attach a negative label to yourself, or you allow others to do so. Without knowing it, you begin to play in ways that are consistent with the label.

Thinking about What You Don't Want to Do: You think in terms of what you don't want to do. This creates confusion. To end the uncertainty, your brain disregards the "don't." "Don't hook it," becomes "Hook it."

Examples of Faulty Thinking Patterns

A faulty thinking pattern that develops inside your head on the golf course can lead to big problems. It's important that you become skilled at identifying the faulty pattern quickly. Let's take some time to practice. In each of the following examples, note the faulty thinking pattern.

1. You've just tried to go for the green instead of laying up. Unfortunately, the ball landed in a lake. Instead of determining what went wrong with your swing, you start attacking yourself with the following thoughts: "What a terrible decision. What's wrong with me? I'm such a hack. How can I be so brainless?"

    A. Self-Criticism

    B. Binocular Thinking

    C. Thinking in the Future or the Past

D. Perfectionism

   E. Labeling

   F. Thinking about What You Don't Want to Do

2. You duck-hook your tee shot on the second hole. Instead of accepting the shot and then focusing on how to recover, you start remembering other times when you duck-hooked your tee shot. You carefully relive each of those shots, over and over. Later in the round, after sinking a 40-foot putt to save par, you have the following thoughts: "There wasn't much break in it. The greens are in great shape, so the ball is staying on line. Anyway, every golfer gets lucky now and then."

   A. Self-Criticism

   B. Binocular Thinking

   C. Thinking in the Future or the Past

   D. Perfectionism

   E. Labeling

   F. Thinking about What You Don't Want to Do

3. As you prepare to hit an approach shot into a green protected in front by a creek, you tell yourself, "Be sure to not come up short." Before you tee off on a par-three hole, you notice a deep bunker on the right side of the green. The pin is also right. Your thoughts: "Don't go right. No matter what, don't go right."

   A. Self-Criticism

   B. Binocular Thinking

   C. Thinking in the Future or the Past

   D. Perfectionism

   E. Labeling

F. Thinking about What You Don't Want to Do

4. As you prepare to hit your approach shot on the tenth hole, you find yourself thinking about the creek that runs along the thirteenth and fourteenth fairways. You're thinking about how difficult those holes will play. "I sure hope I can par them," you say to yourself. "If not, this is going to be a bad round." You make the turn at six over par. As you walk up to the tenth tee, your thoughts wander back to the front nine. It's your turn to hit, but all you can think about are the mistakes you've already made.

   A. Self-Criticism

   B. Binocular Thinking

   C. Thinking in the Future or the Past

   D. Perfectionism

   E. Labeling

   F. Thinking about What You Don't Want to Do

5. Instead of enjoying the round and playing one shot at a time, you decide that you want to play your best round of the season. Your expectations include no double bogies and no three-putts. You also expect to hit twelve fairways and fifteen greens. After six holes, you're four over par and boiling inside. From this point forward, you will have to play without making a single error.

   A. Self-Criticism

   B. Binocular Thinking

   C. Thinking in the Future or the Past

   D. Perfectionism

   E. Labeling

   F. Thinking about What You Don't Want to Do

6. You finish a round in which you hit few fairways and even fewer greens. You start to think of yourself as a bogey golfer. The voice inside your head says, "You're a bogey golfer. It's your fate. You might as well accept it. Pars will be few and far between. Bogey golfers always shoot in the nineties and that's the best you can do."

   A. Self-Criticism

   B. Binocular Thinking

   C. Thinking in the Future or the Past

   D. Perfectionism

   E. Labeling

   F. Thinking about What You Don't Want to Do

7. You slice an approach shot out of bounds and make a point of telling yourself, and all three of your playing partners, what a bad shot it was. A couple of holes later, you're still ruminating about the shot. After the round ends, you go into the clubhouse and describe the shot to several of your friends.

   A. Self-Criticism

   B. Binocular Thinking

   C. Thinking in the Future or the Past

   D. Perfectionism

   E. Labeling

   F. Thinking about What You Don't Want to Do

8. Your five-iron approach shot hits your target but rolls seven feet past the pin. You expected the ball to land softly and then check up below the hole. Your putt is on line, but comes up two inches

short. You start to fume. You expect your approach shots to be stiff, and you expect to make every short putt.

   A. Self-Criticism

   B. Binocular Thinking

   C. Thinking in the Future or the Past

   D. Perfectionism

   E. Labeling

   F. Thinking about What You Don't Want to Do

9. After leaving a couple of putts short, you tell yourself that you're a spineless human being unworthy of being on a golf course. Because you're such a coward, maybe you ought to give up golf and try something that doesn't require courage, maybe gardening. Wimp!

   A. Self-Criticism

   B. Binocular Thinking

   C. Thinking in the Future or the Past

   D. Perfectionism

   E. Labeling

   F. Thinking about What You Don't Want to Do

10. The landing area for your tee shot is narrow, and the fairway slopes left. Trees line the left side of the fairway, as well. Just before making your swing, you say to yourself, "Be sure to not hit a hook."

    A. Self-Criticism

    B. Binocular Thinking

    C. Thinking in the Future or the Past

    D. Perfectionism

E. Labeling

F. Thinking about What You Don't Want to Do

11. You just hit your tee shot well to the right of the fairway. As you walk off the tee, you whisper to yourself, "I'm a slicer. I've always been a slicer. Once you're a slicer, you can never change." You're convinced that this will always be the case.

    A. Self-Criticism

    B. Binocular Thinking

    C. Thinking in the Future or the Past

    D. Perfectionism

    E. Labeling

    F. Thinking about What You Don't Want to Do

12. As you begin to study a putt, your thoughts wander back to the great seven-iron shot you made on the previous hole. You're thinking that you would like to get all your approach shots that close. Dwelling on that shot is making you feel really good about your game.

    A. Self-Criticism

    B. Binocular Thinking

    C. Thinking in the Future or the Past

    D. Perfectionism

    E. Labeling

    F. Thinking about What You Don't Want to Do

Answers:

1. A—Self-Criticism

2. B—Binocular Thinking
3. F—Thinking About What You Don't Want to Do
4. C—Thinking in the Future or the Past
5. D—Perfectionism
6. E—Labeling
7. B—Binocular Thinking
8. D—Perfectionism
9. A—Self-Criticism
10. F—Thinking About What You Don't Want to Do
11. E—Labeling
12. C—Thinking in the Future or the Past

Step Two: Replace the Distorted Thoughts

Once you've identified the faulty thinking pattern, you're ready for Step Two of the procedure: Replace the Distorted Thoughts. First, I'll demonstrate how to replace distorted thoughts. A little later, it will be your turn. To make learning a little easier, we will use some examples from the previous section.

Example One

Distorted Thoughts: You've just tried to go for the green instead of laying up. Unfortunately, the ball landed in a lake. Instead of determining what went wrong with your swing, you start attacking yourself with the following thoughts: "What a terrible decision. What's wrong with me? I'm such a hack. How can I be so brainless?"

Faulty Thinking Pattern: Self-Criticism

Replace the Distorted Thoughts: Having identified the faulty thinking pattern as self-criticism, you now realize that you need to focus your attention on your game, not your personality. Remind yourself that you took the time to evaluate the risks and rewards of the shot. And, after careful consideration, you decided to take a gamble. Yes, you would like to have the shot over, but that's not possible now. Tell yourself that the outcome of the shot has nothing to do with your intelligence; the problem occurred with your swing. As the club head was traveling through the impact zone, it was moving from the outside to the inside. This caused you to slice the ball. Make up your mind that for the rest of the round you will talk to yourself in a positive and encouraging manner.

Example Two

Distorted Thoughts: You duck-hook your tee shot on the second hole. Instead of accepting the shot and then focusing on how to recover, you start remembering other times when you duck-hooked your tee shot. You carefully relive each of those shots, over and over. Later in the round, after sinking a 40-foot putt to save par, you have the following thoughts: "There wasn't much break in it. The greens are in great shape, so the ball is staying on line. Anyway, every golfer gets lucky now and then."

Faulty Thinking Pattern: Binocular Thinking

Replace the Distorted Thoughts: Binocular thinking indicates that you are magnifying your bad shots and minimizing your good ones. As you know, this will lower your confidence. Regarding the tee shot, tell yourself in an authoritative voice to stop dwelling on it. Next, recall a successful tee shot that you recently made, and replay that shot in your head a couple of times. Pay attention to the details. With respect to the putt, remind yourself that you took the time to accurately judge the line and the speed. You stroked the ball smoothly, and the result was exactly what you planned. Relive this putt in your head right now and several more times during the round. Remember, magnify your good shots and minimize your bad ones. That was an outstanding putt!

Example Three

Distorted Thoughts: As you prepare to hit an approach shot into a green protected in front by a creek, you tell yourself, "Be sure to not come up short." Before you tee off on a par-three hole, you notice a deep bunker on the right side of the green. The pin is also right. Your thoughts: "Don't go right. No matter what, don't go right."

Faulty Thinking Pattern: Thinking About What You Don't Want to Do

Replace the Distorted Thoughts: You're not ready to make this shot because you haven't decided what shot you want to play. Back off from the ball and start over at the beginning of your pre-shot routine. Decide on the shot you're going to play, and then give your mind exact instructions on how to play it. For example, "Play a slight draw to the middle of the green. The right club is a six-iron. Be sure to stay behind the ball until you finish your follow-through. The target is the exact middle of the green." Now you're ready.

Example Four

Distorted Thoughts: As you prepare to hit your approach shot on the tenth hole, you find yourself thinking about the creek that runs along the thirteenth and fourteenth fairways. You're thinking about how difficult those holes will play. "I sure hope I can par them," you say to yourself. "If not, this could turn into a bad round."

Faulty Thinking Pattern: Thinking in the Future

Replace the Distorted Thoughts: Recognize that your thoughts have wandered into the future. You're thinking about things that are not related to the shot at hand. As a result, your concentration is divided, and your chances for making a successful shot plummet. Back off from the ball, take a couple of deep breaths, and then focus all of your attention in the present moment. Focus on the important aspects of this shot. Think about the process, not the outcome. Now you're ready to make a quality golf shot.

Example Five

Distorted Thoughts: Instead of enjoying the round and playing one shot at a time, you decide that you want to play your best round of the season. Your expectations include no double bogies and no three-putts. You also expect to hit twelve fairways and fifteen greens. After six holes, you're four over par and boiling inside. From this point forward, you will have to play without making a single error.

Faulty Thinking Pattern: Perfectionism

Replace the Distorted Thoughts: Tell yourself that you're thinking like a perfectionist. Even Tiger Woods would have a difficult time meeting those expectations. Acknowledge that making four bogies in six holes is not exactly stellar golf, and that you're capable of playing much better. Adjust your expectations so that they are consistent with your skills, eight fairway and eleven greens. This will remove the unnecessary pressure you're putting on yourself. Finally, direct the energy stemming from your frustration into improving your course management and club selection.

Example Six

Distorted Thoughts: You finish a round in which you hit few fairways and even fewer greens. You start to think of yourself as a bogey golfer. The voice inside your head is saying, "You're a bogey golfer. It's your fate. You might as well accept it. Pars will be few and far between. Bogey golfers always shoot in the nineties and that's the best you can do."

Faulty Thinking Pattern: Labeling

Replace the Distorted Thoughts: You've just attached a label to yourself that will negatively affect the way you play. Reject the label outright. It's true that you had a bad round, but every golfer has bad rounds, and every golfer is not a bogey golfer. Recall that you were six over on your last round. Dwell on that round for a while. Decide that during the upcoming week you'll spend some time at the practice range making the necessary adjustments to your swing. Finally, identify one part of your game that is going well, and think about that on your way home from the course.

Test Your Skills

When you're on the golf course and your thinking gets off track it's important to take corrective action right away. First, identify the faulty thinking pattern. Second, replace the distorted thoughts. The following illustrations are designed to test your skills at the important two-step procedure. When you're finished, you can check your responses with mine.

Illustration One

Distorted Thoughts: You pull a wedge shot and say to yourself, "I can't believe I missed the green from here. It's the biggest green on the golf course. What's wrong with me? I'm such a terrible player. As you walk down the fairway, you continue, "There is no excuse; when it comes to having a short game, I am totally inept. I have no talent."

Identify the Faulty Thinking Pattern

Replace the Distorted Thoughts

Illustration Two

Distorted Thoughts: You're getting ready to hit your tee shot on a par-five hole. You know that if you hit a long drive, you can get home in two. As you stick your tee into the ground, you tell yourself, "Be sure to not overswing. Whatever you do, don't overswing."

Identify the Faulty Thinking Pattern

Replace the Distorted Thoughts

Illustration Three

Distorted Thoughts: It's the annual club championship. You're keyed up and want to play your best. On the practice range, minutes before you're scheduled to tee off, you tell yourself, "To win this tournament I will have to play one of the best rounds of my life. I'll need to hit at least eleven fairways and fourteen greens. There is no room for mistakes. Everything must go exactly as planned."

Identify the Faulty Thinking Pattern

Replace the Distorted Thoughts

Illustration Four

Distorted Thoughts: Your thoughts, after going bogey, par, double bogey, birdie, "I wish I could play more consistently, but I can't. I'm an inconsistent player. I always played inconsistently and I always will. There's no way around it. I just have to accept it. That's the kind of player I am."

Identify the Faulty Thinking Pattern

Replace the Distorted Thoughts

Illustration Five

Distorted Thoughts: Your company is hosting a golf outing, and you're next up on the first tee. A large group of co-workers and clients stands nearby. Instead of thinking about what you need to do to hit a good first drive, you think about all the things that might go wrong during the round. Someone told you that the back nine plays especially tough. You're feeling anxious about how you will score on those holes.

Identify the Faulty Thinking Pattern

Replace the Distorted Thoughts

Illustration Six

Distorted Thoughts: You hit an extra-long, extra-straight tee shot. Instead of enjoying the accomplishment and building on your success, you explain it away. "It must be that new type of ball I'm playing. The salesperson said that it would add fifteen yards to my tee shots." After your next long and straight drive, you comment, "The salesperson was right. This ball has turned me into a big hitter. I think I'll stop on the way home and pick up a couple dozen."

Identify the Faulty Thinking Pattern

Replace the Distorted Thoughts

Now it's time to check your responses with mine.

Illustration One

This is an example of self-criticism. I would replace the distorted thoughts by saying, "This is not the time or the place for a personality assessment. I'm having some difficulty with my short game. It's time to focus my attention on what is wrong with my swing mechanics. Once I identify the problem, I'll make the necessary adjustments. Continuing to make disparaging remarks about my character will only make matters worse." If you're not successful at making the swing correction on the course, decide that you will grab a bucket of balls and practice wedge shots after the round.

Illustration Two

You're thinking in terms of what not to do. The message you just gave yourself will translate to "Be sure to overswing, whatever you do, overswing." It's time to get back to thinking straight. Tell yourself what you want to do, using exact instructions. For example, "I'm going to hit a solid drive here. I'm going to stay balanced, make a full shoulder turn, accelerate through the ball, and hit a soft draw."

Illustration Three

You're thinking like a perfectionist. This faulty thinking pattern will cause your performance to drop off, not improve. It's natural to feel keyed up. After all, it's a big tournament, you're a competitive person, and you want to play your best. However, be careful. Unreasonable expectations will add more pressure, and you feel more than enough pressure already. Adjust your expectations to realistic levels. For example, "I'm going to play a good round today and manage the course well. I would like to hit eight fairways and eleven greens. More importantly, I'm going to stay relaxed and concentrate completely on every shot."

Illustration Four

Be careful! Quite a bit will go wrong with your golf game when you label yourself an "inconsistent player." If you accept the label, you will begin to play inconsistently. Instead, say to yourself, "The ability to recover after playing a hole poorly is a positive attribute, and I just did it twice. I'm the type of player who stays calm, even when things are not going well. I've always had a lot of composure." Remember, attach positive labels, and reject negative ones.

Illustration Five

You're thinking in the future. This is never a good idea when you have a golf club in your hand. Take a moment and direct your thoughts to the present, to the shot you're preparing to make. Visualize making a great shot. Now, rehearse the swing, and focus on the feel of the club. Keeping your thoughts in the present will help you get off to a good start and keep your nervousness at a minimum.

Illustration Six

You're minimizing your achievements. The explanation that you're hitting long drives because of the new ball will make the manufacturer very happy. However, you're diminishing your skills and missing a great opportunity to build some confidence. Turn the binoculars around, in effect, magnifying the contribution your skills are making. During the remainder of the round, be sure to take some time and dwell on your successful drives.

Chapter Summary

- The human brain uses thinking patterns to process information accurately. On occasion, the complex nature of the brain causes the development of a faulty thinking pattern. When this happens, the brain begins to process information incorrectly.

- When you're on the golf course and a faulty thinking pattern develops inside your head, it can spell big trouble. Instead of keeping things simple, things become complicated. Instead of thinking clearly, your thoughts become distorted. Because thoughts determine feelings, you can no longer trust what you feel. In this frame of mind your performance naturally declines.

- Golfers need to watch for six faulty thinking patterns: self-criticism, binocular thinking, thinking in the future or the past, perfectionism, labeling, and thinking about what you don't want to do.

- When you're on the golf course and your thinking goes awry, a two-step procedure will get you back to thinking straight. In Step One, you identify the faulty thinking pattern. In Step Two, you replace the distorted thoughts with accurate thoughts.

CONCLUSION

If he stands out there until he's ninety, he's not going to improve.
—Ben Hogan

We've come to the end of the book. I hope you have enjoyed reading it as much as I have enjoyed writing it. Before we close, I want to leave you with one final thought:

Golf is a much easier game than you think. That's right, much easier.

Perhaps you disagree. If you're like many players, you've spent a lot of time diligently working to improve your game. And yet, try as you may, you never feel truly satisfied. You never become the player you think you could be. The reason for your lack of success is not that golf is difficult. The reason is that you are going about it the wrong way.

Ben Hogan and Bobby Jones are a study in contrasts. While both are considered to be in the handful of greatest players of all time, their methods of achieving success could not be more dissimilar. Hogan was the quintessential grinder. He began playing golf at age twelve and turned professional at nineteen. From that time on, he practiced and played almost every day. Ben was a workhorse. Few golfers have come close to spending the amount of time he spent developing and refining his swing. When someone asked him for help on improving their game, Hogan would ask them, "How much do you practice?" When the person answered, Ben would quickly say, "Double that." Hogan's work ethic is renowned. Bobby Jones, on the other hand, was the antithesis of a grinder. Jones had many interests outside of golf. He studied electrical engineering at Georgia Tech. He graduated from Harvard with a degree in English Literature. Later, he attended law school at Emory University and then set up a successful law practice. On average, Jones spent about three months per year playing competitive golf. At the ripe old age of twenty-eight, while still an amateur, he retired.

If you look at Hogan's career, it would be easy to conclude that golf is a very difficult game and that success requires a lot of hard work. But Jones's career disproves this. Jones was the best player of his generation even though he practiced and played relatively little. For Jones, the game seemed easy. How could this be?

Fortunately, I discovered the answer. One afternoon, while doing research for this book, I came across a reference to articles Bobby Jones wrote for *Vanity Fair* magazine in the late 1920s and early 1930s. The subject of the articles was the mental side of golf. I immediately set out to find them. With the help of a powerful computer, I located the magazines in, of all places, a library close to my office. The next day I crawled around in the dark, dusty basement of that library, searching for the articles and hoping they would be in readable condition. An hour later, I came across a three-foot-high stack of dusty *Vanity Fair* magazines.

The difference between Hogan and Jones became apparent as I read the articles. In addition to mastering the fundamentals for the physical side of golf, Jones possessed a thorough understanding of the mental side of the game. Hogan probably had greater mastery of the physical side of golf, but tended to overlook the mental side. And this, I believe, is what made golf a much easier game for Jones. Take the time to master the fundamentals of the mental side of golf and I'm certain that you find golf a much easier game as well.

By the way, alligators aren't the only animals that make good golfers. There's a tiger out there right now who is on the prowl.

BIBLIOGRAPHY

1. Ballesteros, Seve. *Natural Golf.* New York: Macmillan Publishing Co., 1988.

2. Couples, Fred. "Back in the Swing." *The Golfer*, 1996: 50–54.

3. Floyd, Raymond. *The Elements of Scoring.* New York: Simon and Schuster, 1998.

4. Hogan, Ben. *Five Lessons The Modern Fundamentals of Golf.* New York: A.S. Barnes and Co., 1957.

5. Jones, Robert. *Bobby Jones on Golf.* New York: Doubleday, 1966.

6. Jones, Robert. "Some Practical Hints on the Art of Putting." *Vanity Fair.* 1930, April, 76–108.

7. Jones, Robert. "The Mental Side of Golf." *Vanity Fair*, 1928, September, 75–115.

8. Marieb, Elainenicpon. *Essentials of Human Anatomy and Physiology.* Fifth Edition. Menlo Park, CA: The Benjamin/Cummings Publishing Co., Inc., 1997.

9. Nicklaus, Jack. *Golf My Way.* New York: Simon Schuster, 1974.

10. Norman, Greg. *Greg Norman's Instant Lessons.* New York: Simon and Schuster, 1993.

11. Norman, Greg. *Shark Attack.* New York: Simon and Schuster, 1988.

12. Palmer, Arnold. *Play Great Golf.* New York: Doubleday and Co., Inc., 1987.

13. Palmer, Arnold. *My Game and Yours.* New York: Simon and Schuster, 1963.

14. Penick, Harvey. *Harvey Penick's Little Red Book.* New York: Simon and Schuster, 1992.

15. Snead, Sam. *The Game I Love.* New York: Ballantine Books, 1997.

16. Snead, Sam. *The Lessons I've Learned.* New York: Macmillan Publishing Co., 1989.

17. Strange, Curtis. *Win and Win Again.* Chicago, IL: Contemporary Books, 1990.

18. Watson, Tom. *Getting Up and Down.* New York: Random House, 1987.

19. Woods, Tiger. *How I Play Golf.* New York: Warner Books, 2001.

978-0-595-39626-9
0-595-39626-7

Printed in the United Kingdom
by Lightning Source UK Ltd.
122872UK00001B/435/A